The Nature Kid's Guide to

BATS

DAVID ANDERSON

LP Media Inc. Publishing

For information address LP Media Inc. Publishing,
30012 Variolite St NW, Princeton MN 55371
www.lpmedia.org

Publication Data

Bats
The Nature Kid's Guide to Bats — First edition.

Summary: "Learn all about Bats, the Nature Kid Way"
— Provided by publisher.

ISBN: 979-8-89818-190-1

[1. Bats – Non-Fiction] I. Title.

Title: The Nature Kid's Guide to Bats

CONTENTS

BRILLIANT BATS

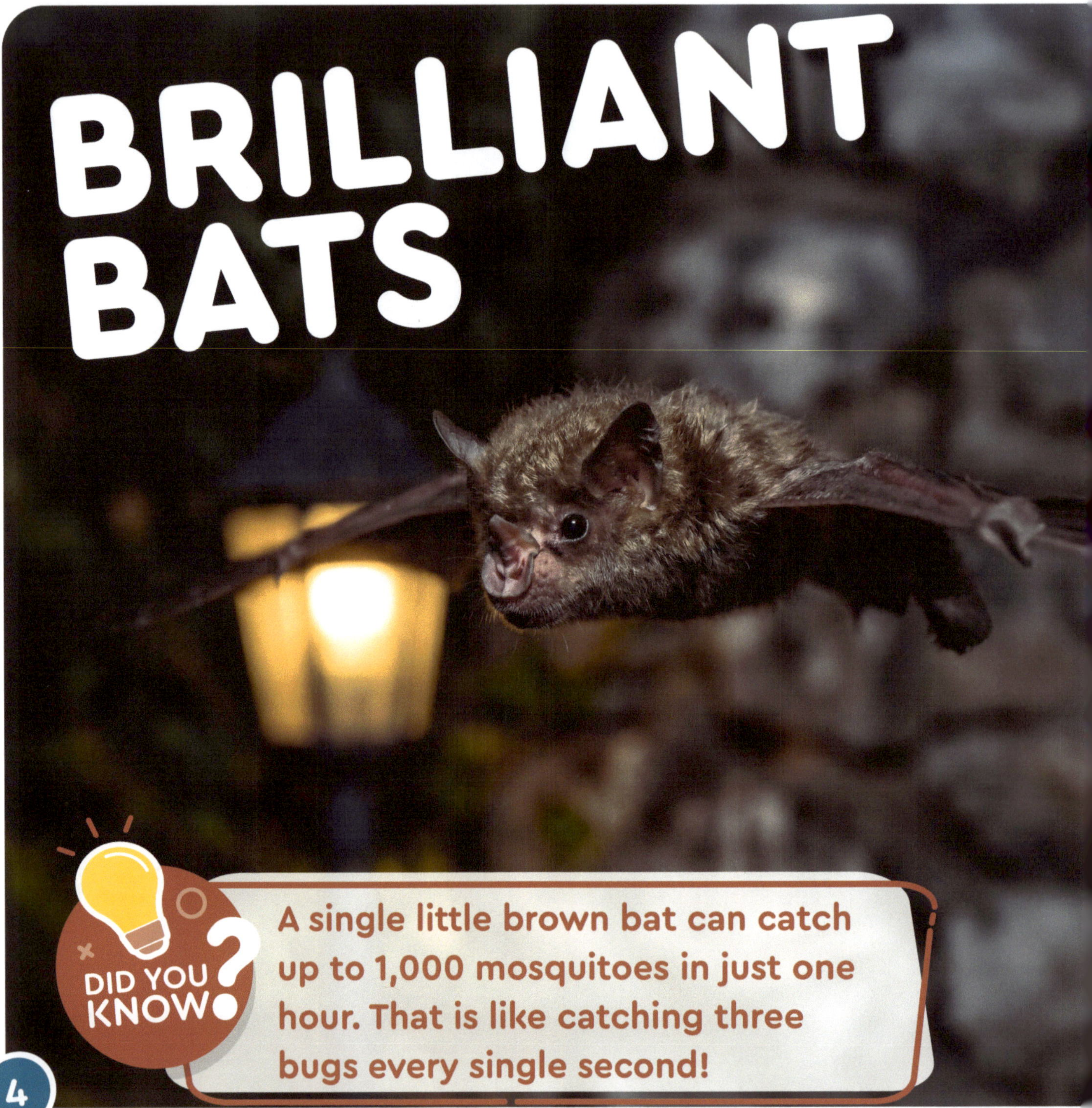

DID YOU KNOW?

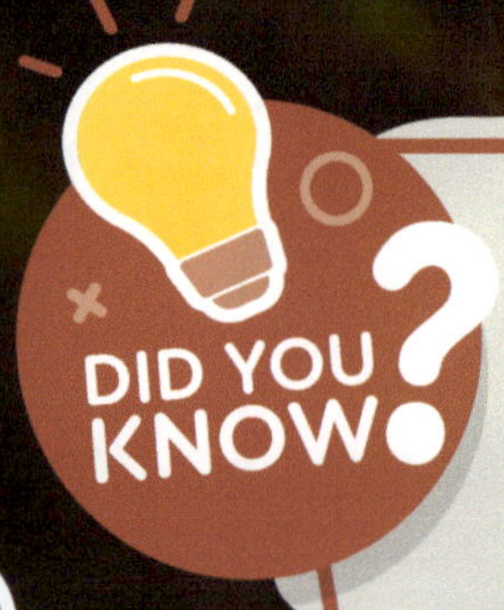

A single little brown bat can catch up to 1,000 mosquitoes in just one hour. That is like catching three bugs every single second!

Swoosh! A dark shape zooms past your head at night.

Bats are the only mammals that can truly fly. Not glide and drift, but flap their wings and soar! Over 1,400 kinds live on every continent except Antarctica.

Some bats are tiny. The bumblebee bat weighs less than a penny and fits right in your palm. Others, like the giant flying fox, spread wings wider than most kids are tall.

Bats are hard workers too. One bat can eat thousands of mosquitoes in a single night. Fruit bats plant forests by dropping seeds wherever they fly.

WING
WONDERS

Flap, flap! A bat stretches its long, thin wings wide.

A bat's wing is not like a bird's wing. Thin skin stretches between its long finger bones. This helps it twist and turn fast in the air — even faster than most birds can.

Bats have strong back legs too. They use them to hang upside down for hours. Sharp claws grip bark and rock tight.

Big ears help bats hear well. Soft fur keeps them warm at night. Every part of a bat is made for life in the dark.

A bat's thumb has a tiny claw that helps it climb, grip food, and groom its fur.

SONIC HEARING

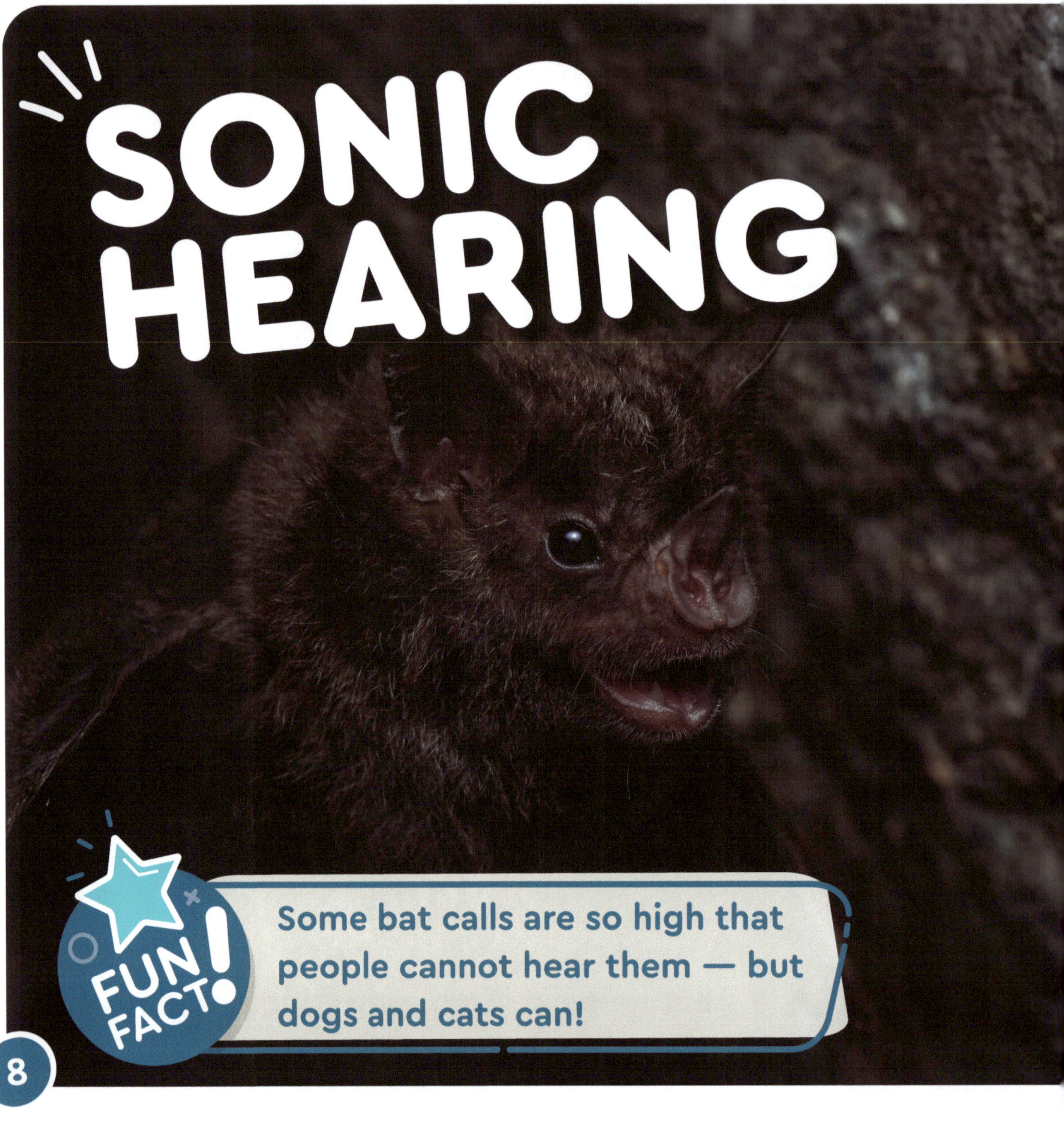

Some bat calls are so high that people cannot hear them — but dogs and cats can!

Click, click, click! A bat calls out into the darkness.

Most bats use sound to find their way. They send out high calls that bounce off things. The echo comes back and tells them what is near. This amazing skill is called **echolocation**.

It happens super fast — up to 200 calls per second! A bat can tell where a moth is. It can even tell how big it is. All from the echo of one tiny call!

Some bats call through their mouth. Others call through their nose. Each kind of bat has its own special sound.

HUNGRY HUNTERS

Some bats use their wing like a baseball mitt to scoop bugs right into their mouth!

Snap! A bat snatches a mosquito right out of the air.

One hungry bat can eat hundreds of bugs in a single night! Moths, beetles, and other insects don't stand a chance. Bats are some of the best hunters in the sky.

Some bats love fruit instead. They bite into ripe pieces and sip the sweet juice. Hammer-headed bats have big lips made just for this messy job.

A few bats hunt even bigger prey, like fish, frogs, or other bats. These hunters use sharp ears, good eyes, and strong noses to track down a meal.

HANGING HIDEOUTS

Shh! Thousands of Ghost bats hang still inside a dark cave.

Bats need a safe place to sleep during the day. This resting spot is called a **roost**. Caves, old trees, and bridges all make good roosts.

When winter comes, some bats hibernate. They slow their bodies way down and sleep for months until bugs return. That is one very long nap!

Other species tuck into hollow trees or under loose bark. Ghost bats love deep, dark caves best.

Hibernating bats drop their heart rate from 400 beats per minute to just 25!

BATTY BUDDIES

Squeak, squeak! A vampire bat calls out to his friends nearby.

Bats are incredibly social animals. Many live in **colonies** holding millions of bats packed together. The heat from so many bodies keeps the whole group warm and safe.

Bats know their colony mates by voice and smell. They groom each other and keep track of who is who even in a crowd of thousands.

Vampire bats take friendship even further. When one comes home hungry, a colony mate shares its meal, and that bat will return the favor later.

Some bat nurseries hold millions of pups – That's what baby bats are called!

BACKYARD BATS

Flutter! A little brown bat zips past a garden light.

Little brown bats are common in North America. They are tiny, about the size of a mouse and weighing less than half an ounce. Soft brown fur helps them blend into tree bark.

These bats love to hunt near water. They swoop low and grab bugs right off the surface. A single bat can fill its belly in about an hour.

In fall, they fly to caves to sleep through winter. Little brown bats can live more than 30 years. That is a very long life for such a small animal!

FLYING FOXES

Crunch! A fruit bat bites into a juicy, ripe mango.

Fruit bats are some of the biggest bats in the world. The largest ones are called flying foxes, and their wings can stretch five feet wide! Their faces look a bit like a fox, and that is how they got their name.

These bats use big eyes to spot ripe fruit at night. A strong nose helps too. Unlike most bats, they do not use echolocation at all.

Fruit bats rest in treetops by day. They hang in huge groups called camps. Some camps hold thousands of bats, all chattering and jostling for the best spots.

VAMPIRE VISITORS

20

Shhh! A vampire bat creeps closer on the dark ground.

Vampire bats are the only bats that feed on blood. They live in warm parts of Central and South America. These small bats hunt at night while other animals sleep.

A vampire bat lands near its target quietly. Then it walks on the ground using its strong arms. Its razor-sharp teeth make a tiny cut, and it laps up the blood with its tongue.

The bite does not hurt much. The bat's spit has something special that keeps blood flowing. But don't worry — the bat only drinks about two tablespoons, then he leaves.

TINY TITANS

A bumblebee bat's body is only about one inch long — smaller than your thumb!

Perch! The world's smallest bat fits on the end of your finger!

The Kitti's hognosed bat is the smallest bat on Earth. Most people call it the bumblebee bat because it is about the same size as a big bumblebee! This tiny creature weighs about as much as a penny, just 2 grams.

This little bat lives in caves in Thailand and Myanmar. It comes out at dusk to catch small bugs near the treetops. Each hunt lasts only about 30 minutes.

Bumblebee bats are very rare. Only a few caves are home to them. People are working hard to keep these little bats safe for the future.

PHANTOM PREDATOR

Ghost bats are sometimes called false vampire bats — but they never drink blood!

Swoop! A pale ghost bat drops down onto its prey below.

Ghost bats get their name from their pale, thin wings. You can almost see right through them! These bats are not gentle fruit eaters. They are fierce hunters that go after other animals.

They live in northern Australia, roosting in dark caves and old mines during the day. At night, they use sharp eyes and huge ears to track down prey in the darkness.

When a ghost bat spots a meal, it drops from above like a silent dive-bomber. Frogs, lizards, and even mice are all on the menu. Their strong jaws grab hold and do not let go until the fight is over.

HORSESHOE HUNTERS

Ping! A horseshoe bat sends a call out through its nose.

Horseshoe bats have a funny flap of skin on their nose. It looks just like a horseshoe! This odd flap helps them aim their echolocation calls.

These bats live in Europe, Asia, and Africa. They hunt in dark forests and along quiet rivers. Moths and beetles are their favorite meals.

When horseshoe bats rest, they wrap their wings around their body like a blanket. They look like small, fuzzy pods hanging from the cave roof. This keeps them warm and hidden.

There are more than 100 kinds of horseshoe bats — and scientists keep finding new ones!

SPOTTED SECRETS

Spotted bat calls are so low that people can actually hear them — they sound like tiny clicks!

Squeak! A spotted bat shows off its bold black and white fur.

Spotted bats are easy to spot! They have three big white spots on their black fur. Their pink ears are the biggest of any bat in North America — almost as long as their body.

These bats live in the western United States and Mexico. They like dry, rocky places with tall cliffs. At night, they hunt high in the sky for moths.

Spotted bats are hard to find and study. They roost alone in cracks on high cliffs. Scientists are still learning their secrets.

FISHING PHANTOM

FUN FACT!

Fishing bats have pouches in their cheeks to store fish while flying back to their roost!

Splash! A fishing bat drags its claws through the water.

Fishing bats have a special trick. They fly low over water and drag sharp claws along the surface. When they feel a fish bump their feet, they grab it!

These bats live near rivers and coasts in Central and South America. Their big feet and long, hooked claws are perfect for snatching slippery fish.

Fishing bats also eat bugs that fly near the water. They use echolocation to find tiny ripples that fish make when they swim near the surface.

PAINTED PERFECTION

DID YOU KNOW?

Painted bats are so tiny that they can curl up inside a matchbox!

Rustle! A painted bat shows of its bright and colorful wings.

Painted bats are nature's colorful surprise. Their fur is bright orange. Their wings are black and orange. They look almost too pretty to be real!

These small bats live in forests across southern Asia. They hide inside curled, dry leaves during the day. Their bright colors actually help them blend in with dead leaves on the ground.

At night, painted bats flutter quietly through the forest catching small bugs. They are so shy and secretive that even scientists have a hard time studying them. That makes every sighting of these little beauties extra special.

BIZARRE BATS

Honk! A hammer-headed bat calls out in an African forest.

The hammer-headed bat is one of the oddest-looking bats in the world. It lives in the tropical forests of Africa. Males have a huge, heavy head with big, floppy lips and a swollen nose that looks like no other bat on Earth.

Males honk loudly at night to call for a mate. They sound more like frogs than bats! They line up along rivers in big groups, each one honking as loud as it can, hoping a female will pick them.

Hammer-headed bats are the largest bats in Africa. They eat fruit, using their big eyes and strong noses to find ripe figs in the dark. Despite their strange looks, they are gentle fruit lovers.

BATTLING EXTINCTION

Crack! A tree falls, and a bat colony loses its home.

Many bats around the world are in trouble. When people cut down trees, bats lose their homes. Filling in caves and bright lights can scare bats away from their roosts.

A terrible sickness called white-nose syndrome has killed millions of bats in North America. A fuzzy white mold grows on their noses while they **hibernate**. It wakes them up too soon, and they starve.

But people can help! They can put up bat houses and keep caves safe. Without bats, there would be way too many bugs. Farms and gardens need bats.

BAT FANS

In Austin, Texas, crowds of 100,000 people gather each summer to watch 1.5 million bats fly out from under a bridge!

Whoosh! A sky full of bats streams out at sunset to explore.

Bats are some of nature's best helpers. They move pollen from flower to flower. Many fruits we eat — like bananas and mangoes — come from plants that bats help grow.

People all over the world love bats. Some towns hold bat festivals. Others gather to watch huge groups of bats stream out at sunset, filling the sky like a dark, swirling river.

You can be a bat fan too! Learn about the bats near your home. Tell your friends why bats matter. The more we know about these amazing flyers, the more we can help them soar.

GLOSSARY

mammal
A warm-blooded animal that feeds its babies milk.

echolocation
Using sound echoes to find things in the dark.

roost
A safe place where bats rest and sleep.

hibernate
To sleep deeply through winter to save energy.

colonies
A large group of bats living together.